Level B • Book 2

QuickReads®
A Research-Based Fluency Program

Elfrieda H. Hiebert, Ph.D.

MODERN CURRICULUM PRESS

Pearson Learning Group

Program Reviewers and Consultants

Dr. Barbara A. Baird
Director of Federal Programs/Richardson ISD
Richardson, TX

Dr. Kate Kinsella
Dept. of Secondary Education and Step to College Program
San Francisco State University
San Francisco, CA

Pat Sears
Early Child Coordinator/Virginia Beach Public Schools
Virginia Beach, VA

Dr. Judith B. Smith
Supervisor of ESOL and World and Classical Languages/Baltimore City Public Schools
Baltimore, MD

The following people have contributed to the development of this product:

Art and Design: Adriano Farinella, Dorothea Fox, Salita Mehta, Janice Noto-Helmers, Evelyn O'Shea, Dan Thomas

Editorial: Lynn W. Kloss

Manufacturing: Michele Uhl

Marketing: Connie Buck

Production: Laura Benford-Sullivan, Jeffrey Engel

Publishing Operations: Jennifer Van Der Heide

Modern Curriculum Press
Pearson Learning Group

1-800-321-3106
www.pearsonlearning.com

Contents

Contents

Contents

SCIENCE **Water and Us**

Contents

Acknowledgments

All photographs © Pearson Learning unless otherwise noted.

Cover: Getty Images, Inc.

Interior: 3: © WorldSat International/Photo Researchers, Inc. 4: Esbin/Anderson/Omni-Photo Communications, Inc. 6: Tony Freeman/PhotoEdit. 7: Daphne Carew/Gallo Images/Corbis. 8: Aaron Horowitz/Corbis. 10: © WorldSat International/Photo Researchers, Inc. 24: Esbin/Anderson/Omni-Photo Communications, Inc. 26: Jack Fields/ Corbis. 30: Andy Sotiriou/PhotoDisc, Inc./Getty Images, Inc. 32: David Young-Wolff/PhotoEdit. 38: © 1977, VCG/FPG International LLC/Getty Images, Inc. 42: © Lawrence Migdale. 42: Tom Stack for Silver Burdett Ginn. 44: Bonnie Kamin/PhotoEdit. 46: Mary Kate Denny/PhotoEdit. 52: Tony Freeman/PhotoEdit. 54: Myrleen Ferguson/PhotoEdit. 56: Geostock/Photo Disc, Inc./Getty Images, Inc. 58: The Superior Daily Telegram/AP/Wide World Photos. 60: t. B. Stitzer/PhotoEdit; b. George H. Harrison/Grant Heilman Photography, Inc. 66: David Young-Wolff/PhotoEdit. 68: Daphne Carew/Gallo Images/Corbis. 70: © Ezio Geneletti/The Image Bank/Getty Images. 74: Laura Rubin/The Image Bank/Getty Images, Inc. 80: Keith S. Walklet/Quietworks. 82: Eric Kroll/Omni-Photo Communications, Inc. 84: Aaron Horowitz/Corbis. 86: Kevin Schafer/Corbis.

Maps

North and South America

This map of North and South America looks like it was drawn from a plane.

What Is a Map?

A map is a small drawing of a place. It does not matter how big the place is. The map will[25] fit on one piece of paper. A map of your school with all of its classrooms and halls could fit on one piece of paper.[50] Even if a town is big, a map of the town will fit on one piece of paper.

Most maps show places from above, as[75] if you were seeing them from a plane. Maps help people find their way around places. With a map, you can find your way around a new place.[103]

Maps

A map can help your friends
find their way to your house.

A Map to Your House

If new friends are coming to your home, you might give them a map. What would you need to put[25] on your map so that your friends don't get lost?

Your map should have the place where you live, your street, and the names of[50] streets around it. You should put well-known places like a park or a big store on your map, too. These well-known places will[75] help your friends find your house. When they see the real places that you put on the map, your friends will know they are going the right way.[103]

Maps

This map key shows the things
that are in the park.

Keys to Maps

You know about keys that unlock locks. Maps have keys, too. Keys to maps tell you what kind of information the map[25] shows. People who make maps are called mapmakers. Mapmakers put different information in maps because different kinds of maps have different uses. Map keys help[50] mapmakers show information by using pictures, not words.

A map of a town needs to show important buildings and parks. Map keys often use small[75] pictures to stand for important buildings, parks, and trees. Road maps may have numbers to tell you how far it is from one town to another.[101]

Maps

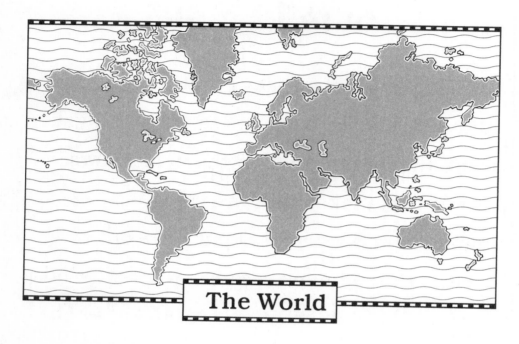

The World

This map of the world shows where
the land and the water are.

Different Maps

When your family goes in a car to a new town, someone most likely uses a road map. A road map shows highways[25] and towns. Another kind of map shows the streets and important buildings in a town.

There are other kinds of maps, too. Maps of the[50] world show where there are large areas of land and water. Other maps of the world show countries, mountains, and rivers. Some maps show how[75] high mountains are. Some maps show how deep seas are. Maps can show many different things about the world. Some maps do all of these things at once.[103]

Maps

This picture was taken from a satellite.
It shows North America and South America.

Mapmaking

Long ago, people thought that the world was flat with a sea around it. They thought people could drop off the end of the[25] flat world. The mapmakers wrote, "Here there be dragons." They put pictures of dragons on the maps to show where they thought the world ended.[50] These mapmakers made mistakes because they did not know the world was round.

The mapmakers of long ago made mistakes like these because they could[75] not see the world from above. Today, pictures taken from satellites and planes help mapmakers draw better maps. From satellites and planes, places can be seen as they really are.[105]

Write words that will help you remember what you learned.

What Is a Map?

_____
_____
_____

A Map to Your House

_____
_____
_____

Keys to Maps

_____
_____
_____

Different Maps

_____
_____
_____

Mapmaking

_____
_____
_____
_____

What Is a Map?

1. The most important idea in "What Is a Map" is _____
   Ⓐ that maps show places in your school.
   Ⓑ that only some maps can fit on one piece of paper.
   Ⓒ that maps are small drawings of a place.
   Ⓓ that maps are drawn on paper.

2. What do maps help people do?

_____

_____

_____

A Map to Your House

1. "A Map to Your House" is MAINLY about _____
   Ⓐ where a park or a big store is.
   Ⓑ how to find a map.
   Ⓒ what a map to your house should show.
   Ⓓ why people use maps.

2. What should a map to your house show?

_____

_____

_____

 **Maps**

Keys to Maps

1. What is on a map key?

  Ⓐ the people who can use the map

  Ⓑ pictures that stand for things on the map

  Ⓒ towns and streets

  Ⓓ the name of the mapmaker

2. Why do mapmakers use map keys?

_____

_____

_____

Different Maps

1. Another good name for "Different Maps" is _____

  Ⓐ "Where to Find Maps."

  Ⓑ "Maps for Cars."

  Ⓒ "Many Kinds of Maps."

  Ⓓ "How People Make Maps."

2. What are three different things maps show?

_____

_____

_____

Mapmaking

1. Why did mapmakers make mistakes long ago?

   Ⓐ They could not see the world from above.

   Ⓑ They did not have good pens or paper.

   Ⓒ They liked to draw dragons.

   Ⓓ Not very many people made maps.

2. How do satellites and planes help mapmakers make better maps today?

   _____

   _____

   _____

Connect Your Ideas

1. Why do you think people started to make maps?

   _____

   _____

   _____

2. Tell about a time your family used a map.

   _____

   _____

   _____

Money

Most times, people trade money for food.

What Is Money?

Today, we use money to pay for the things we need or want. We get money when we are paid for doing[25] something or when we sell something. Long ago, people did not use money like we do today. They traded things. If one person had food[50] and another person had a rug, the food might be traded for a rug.

Sometimes we still trade things like rugs and food for things[75] we want or need. However, most times we use paper money to buy things. This is another kind of trading. We trade money for the things we want or need.[105]

Money

People on one island used
these big stones as money.

Different Kinds of Money

People have used different things for money. Think of rolling a big stone to the store to buy something. If what[25] you wanted cost a lot, you might need to roll more than one big stone. That is what people on one island used to do.[50] They used big, round stones as money.

On another island, people used red feathers for money. The redder the feathers, the more people could buy[75] with them.

Long ago, salt was worth a lot. In some places, people used bars of salt as money. In the United States, the earliest people used beads as money.[105]

Money

The writing and pictures on coins show
that they weigh the right amount.

Coins

A bag of stones can be hard to carry to the store. Many people thought that gold and silver were worth a lot. They[25] began to use gold and silver to pay for things. The people who were selling something would weigh the gold or silver to make sure[50] it was the right amount. Weighing gold and silver takes time.

Gold and silver began to be made into coins. Stamps were put on the[75] coins to show that they weighed the right amount. The stamp was called a mint. A mint is also the name of the place where money is made.[103]

Money

People all over the world use
paper money to buy things.

Paper Money

One hundred gold coins can weigh a lot. It also was not always safe to carry gold and silver. So people began to[25] leave their coins at stores. Storeowners would give people notes to say that they had one hundred coins at the store.

These notes were the[50] first paper money. The paper was not worth much. However, the notes told other storeowners how much money someone had stored. The places where money[75] was stored began to be called banks.

No one sees gold and silver when someone uses paper money. Yet people know that paper money is worth the same as gold and silver.[107]

Money

People can use bankcards as
money when they buy things.

Bankcards

Today, many people don't carry a lot of coins or even paper money with them. They use bankcards. Bankcards are small, plastic cards that[25] computers in stores can read. The computers tell the bank to pay the storeowner for what someone buys in a store. The computers also tell[50] the bank how much the person needs to pay the bank.

Plastic bankcards can be useful. People don't have to carry around lots of coins[75] or paper money. Computers can keep track of lost bankcards. However, bankcards are not money. People need to pay the bank for the things they buy.[101]

Write words that will help you remember what you learned.

What Is Money?

_____

_____

_____

_____

Different Kinds of Money

_____

_____

_____

_____

Coins

_____

_____

_____

_____

Paper Money

_____

_____

_____

_____

Bankcards

_____

_____

_____

_____

What Is Money?

1. Before there was money, how did people pay for things?

   Ⓐ They sold things.

   Ⓑ They made their own things.

   Ⓒ They took what they needed.

   Ⓓ They traded things.

2. How do we use paper money today?

   _____

   _____

   _____

Different Kinds of Money

1. "Different Kinds of Money" is MAINLY about _____

   Ⓐ the different things people have used for money.

   Ⓑ the big stones found in the United States.

   Ⓒ how people trade for things with money.

   Ⓓ how people use salt on their food.

2. Name three things that have been used for money.

   _____

   _____

   _____

 **Money**

Coins

1. Why did people begin to use gold and silver for money?

    Ⓐ People liked the stamps on the money.

    Ⓑ People wanted to see their money.

    Ⓒ People thought that gold and silver were worth a lot.

    Ⓓ People found lots of gold and silver.

2. Why did people make gold and silver into coins?

_____

_____

_____

Paper Money

1. People began using paper money because ____

    Ⓐ paper money weighs less and is safer than gold and silver.

    Ⓑ stores and banks like paper money.

    Ⓒ people did not have gold and silver.

    Ⓓ paper money is not worth much.

2. How did people use the first paper money?

_____

_____

_____

Bankcards

1. What are bankcards?

    Ⓐ paper money that people buy at a store

    Ⓑ plastic cards that people can use like money

    Ⓒ computers that give people money

    Ⓓ plastic cards that a person can buy at a store

2. How do people use bankcards?

_____

_____

_____

Connect Your Ideas

1. What is money?

_____

_____

_____

2. How is the money people use today different from the money people used long ago?

_____

_____

_____

You may not have seen the people
who built your school.

Jobs That Help You

There are many people who do jobs that help you. You see and talk to some of these people, such as[25] your teacher or doctor. Teachers help you learn. Doctors help you stay well.

You don't see all the people who do jobs that help you.[50] You are not likely to see the people who built your school or the writers of the books you read. You are not likely to[75] see the people who make the pens you use to write or the paper on which you write. Around the world, many people are doing jobs that help you.[104]

Jobs Around Us

Police officers help keep people safe.

Keeping Us Safe

Police officers work hard to keep towns and cities safe. They help when there are accidents. Police officers also try to stop[25] accidents. They make sure that people don't break rules that might end in an accident.

Firefighters put out fires in buildings, cars, and forests. They[50] save people who are trapped in burning buildings. Firefighters try to stop fires in forests before the fires get to towns.

People who pick up[75] garbage also help keep towns and cities safe. If garbage is not picked up, people can get sick from germs. People work day and night to keep us safe.[104]

Jobs Around Us

Some engineers make games
to play on computers.

Building New Things

Will people ever drive cars in the sky? Will people ever live in houses under the water? No one knows the answers[25] yet. However, there are people who work to find out how new things can be made. These people are engineers.

Engineers know about math and[50] science. Engineers use what they know about math and science to build things. Some engineers make TVs sound better. Engineers also make computer games that[75] are fun to play. Engineers helped build almost everything we use. They make new things that help people. Engineers also make old things work better for people.[102]

Jobs Around Us

Accountants help people
keep track of their money.

Keeping Track of Money

You know most of the people who work at your school. Yet you may never see the accountant. Accountants help your[25] school by keeping track of money. Accountants use computers to keep track of the money that is spent. Accountants also use computers to keep track[50] of the money that a school gets.

If a school needs new books, an accountant makes sure that there is enough money to pay for[75] the books. Accountants make sure that a school is not spending more money than it gets. Accountants also keep track of money for stores and many other places.[103]

Jobs Around Us

Cooks at school help children
by making them lunch.

Bringing Us Food

Think about a lunch at school made of tuna fish sandwiches and glasses of milk. The lunch started with farmers who planted[25] wheat. The wheat was made into flour. The flour was used to make the bread for the sandwich. People went out on boats to catch[50] the tuna. The tuna was cleaned and put into cans.

Farmers took care of the cows. The farmers milked the cows and made sure that[75] the milk did not go bad. Cooks at school made the tuna fish sandwiches and put out the milk. Many people work hard to make the food we eat.[104]

REVIEW Jobs Around Us

Write words that will help you remember what you learned.

Jobs That Help You	Keeping Us Safe
_____	_____
_____	_____
_____	_____
_____	_____

Building New Things	Keeping Track of Money
_____	_____
_____	_____
_____	_____
_____	_____

Bringing Us Food

_____

_____

_____

_____

Jobs That Help You

1. Another good name for "Jobs That Help You" is _____

Ⓐ "Teachers and Doctors."

Ⓑ "Why People Have Jobs."

Ⓒ "People Who Help You."

Ⓓ "How to Become a Doctor."

2. What are some jobs people do to help you that you don't see?

_____

_____

_____

Keeping Us Safe

1. The main idea of "Keeping Us Safe" is that _____

Ⓐ police officers work hard.

Ⓑ people work day and night.

Ⓒ people have to work to keep themselves safe.

Ⓓ many people have jobs to keep us safe.

2. What are two jobs that people do to keep us safe?

_____

_____

_____

Jobs Around Us

Building New Things

1. "Building New Things" is MAINLY about _____
   Ⓐ math and science.
   Ⓑ what engineers do.
   Ⓒ building houses under water.
   Ⓓ how engineers make TVs.

2. What do engineers do?

_____

_____

_____

Keeping Track of Money

1. An accountant is _____
   Ⓐ someone who works at a school.
   Ⓑ someone who keeps track of money.
   Ⓒ someone who builds schools.
   Ⓓ someone who uses a computer.

2. Name two places where accountants work.

_____

_____

_____

Bringing Us Food

1. What is the main idea of "Bringing Us Food"?

   Ⓐ Farmers bring us food.

   Ⓑ Lunch at school might be made of tuna fish and milk.

   Ⓒ Many people help bring us food.

   Ⓓ Many people work very hard.

2. Name three jobs that are needed to make a lunch of tuna fish sandwiches and milk.

   _____

   _____

   _____

Connect Your Ideas

1. What are four jobs people do that help us every day?

   _____

   _____

   _____

2. Which of the jobs you learned about would you like to do? Why?

   _____

   _____

   _____

Weather

The water in clouds can bring rain or snow.

Weather Around You

Wherever you live, there is weather. Weather can be hot or cold. Weather can be dry or wet. The sky can be[25] cloudy or clear. The wind can be blowing or still. On some days, the weather changes from cloudy to clear or from windy to still.[50]

Different things make and change the weather. Air is always moving and makes the wind. The way Earth turns and moves around the sun changes[75] the weather, too. Some places on Earth get more sun and heat than other places. Water also changes the weather. Water makes clouds that can bring rain and snow.[104]

Weather

The wind helps you fly a kite.

Wind

Wind is air that moves. You cannot see wind, but you can see what wind does. When you see leaves move on a tree,[25] you know that the wind is moving the leaves.

Wind moves from places where air is heavy to places where air is light. Cold air[50] is heavy. Warm air is light. When masses of cold air meet masses of warm air, the wind can be strong. It can blow so[75] hard that people cannot walk into the wind. At other times, not even a leaf is moving. Sometimes the wind blows hard enough to let children fly kites.[103]

Fog can make it hard to see
things that are close.

Clouds and Fog

Little drops of water come together in the sky to make clouds. Clouds get bigger and bigger as they soak up water[25] from oceans and lakes. There are many kinds of clouds. How high a cloud is in the sky and its color tells you if it[50] is going to rain or snow.

Fog is a cloud that is close to Earth. Fog and clouds are formed in the same way. When[75] the weather is foggy, you are really inside a cloud. If you have ever been in fog, you know it's hard to see inside a cloud.[101]

Snow can give some people jobs.

Rain or Snow?

Clouds get big as little water drops come together. The water in the clouds gets too heavy to float in the air.[25] The water drops in the clouds start to fall to the ground. If it is not cold on the ground, the water comes down as[50] rain.

When it is cold, the water drops in clouds freeze into bits of ice. These bits of ice are called snow. All snowflakes look[75] the same when they are coming down. They are the same color and have six sides. Yet if you look closely, you will see that no two snowflakes are the same.[106]

Weather

The climate in some places is cold
in winter and warm in summer.

Climate

Weather can change from cloudy to sunny in a day. Yet most places have certain kinds of weather at certain times of the year.[25] A climate is the usual weather of a place over a year.

The climate is different in the middle and southern parts of the United[50] States. In the middle of the country, it snows only in the winter. People who live by the ocean in the southern part of the[75] United States do not often have snow, even in winter. The weather can change during a day, but the climate of a place stays the same year after year.[104]

Weather

Write words that will help you remember what you learned.

Weather Around You

_____

_____

_____

_____

Wind

_____

_____

_____

_____

Clouds and Fog

_____

_____

_____

_____

Rain or Snow?

_____

_____

_____

_____

Climate

_____

_____

_____

_____

Weather Around You

1. What is another good name for "Weather Around You"?

   Ⓐ "Cold Weather"

   Ⓑ "How to Change the Weather"

   Ⓒ "Bad Weather"

   Ⓓ "Many Kinds of Weather"

2. Name two things that can change the weather.

_____

_____

_____

Wind

1. What is wind?

   Ⓐ warm air

   Ⓑ cold air

   Ⓒ air that moves

   Ⓓ air in the spring

2. What makes strong wind?

_____

_____

_____

Clouds and Fog

1. How are clouds and fog formed?

(A) Rain falls from the sky.

(B) Wind makes dark clouds.

(C) Drops of water come together.

(D) Cold and warm air go up into the sky.

2. What is fog?

_____

_____

_____

Rain or Snow?

1. "Rain or Snow?" is MAINLY about _____

(A) how raindrops and snowflakes look.

(B) how rain and snow form.

(C) why rain clouds form.

(D) how much it rains or snows every year.

2. Why does it rain or snow?

_____

_____

_____

Climate

1. The main idea in "Climate" is that _____
   A places have certain kinds of weather at certain times of the year.
   B weather changes quickly.
   C weather does not change very often in lots of places.
   D climates change every year in the United States.

2. What is a climate?

_____

_____

_____

Connect Your Ideas

1. What kind of weather do you like most? Why?

_____

_____

_____

2. What kind of climate do you have where you live?

_____

_____

_____

Water and Us

People need to drink water to stay alive.

Water in Your Life

You may not think that there is any water when you look around your classroom. Yet there is lots of water[25] in your classroom. Like animals and plants, people's bodies are made up mostly of water. Two-thirds of your body is water.

Like animals and[50] plants, people need water to stay alive. People can't live for more than a few days without water. They need to drink about one quart[75] of water each day. People also use water to cook and clean and to grow crops. Many plants and animals live in the water. Water is very important to us.[105]

Water and Us

Most animals need to drink fresh water.

Fresh or Salty?

Almost three-quarters of Earth is water. However, much of Earth's water is the salt water in oceans. While a little salt[25] can make food taste good, salt water isn't good for people to drink. Like people, many animals and plants need fresh water, not salt water.[50] Fresh water is in many lakes and rivers and under the ground.

There is lots of fresh water on Earth, but it is not always[75] where it is needed. In some places, little rain may fall for a year or two. That means there isn't enough water. People need to use fresh water carefully.[104]

The boiling water in this pot is turning into steam.

Water in the Air

You drink about a quart of water every day. You add ice cubes to drinks. Water in a glass and ice[25] cubes look different, but both are forms of water. Water takes a third form, too. This form is water vapor in the air.

Watch carefully[50] when someone in your house boils water on the stove. When the water boils, you will see steam. The steam is water turning into water[75] vapor. You can't see it, but you can feel the water vapor in the air. On hot days, you feel sticky because of the water vapor in the air.[104]

Water and Us

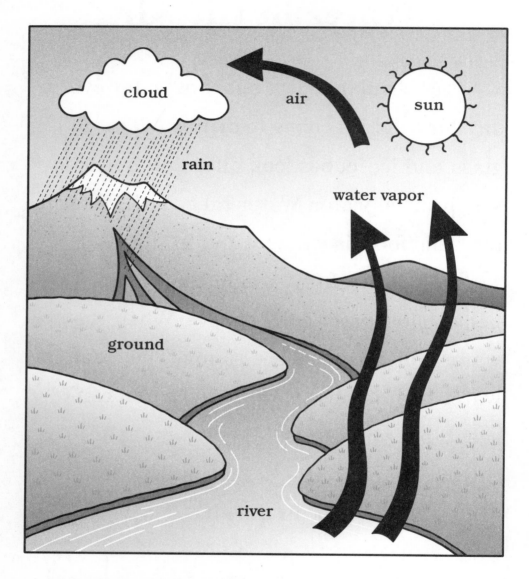

This drawing shows how the water cycle works.

The Water Cycle

Rain that falls from the sky feels clean and new. It may be clean, but it is not new. The water in[25] rain is very old. Water is used again and again on Earth. This use of water is called the water cycle.

The water cycle starts[50] when water in oceans and rivers goes into the air as water vapor. Water vapor turns into clouds. Water falls from the clouds as rain.[75] Some water stays under the ground. Much of the water goes back into the oceans and rivers. Then, the water cycle starts all over again.[100]

Bad chemicals are filtered out of water
before it comes to our homes.

Clean Water

If you have ever added water to a drink, you know that it is easy to mix water with other things. Water can[25] also mix with bad things, such as some chemicals.

Factories and farms sometimes use chemicals. These chemicals can get into the water from the factories[50] and farms. Bad chemicals can hurt plants and animals living in the water. They can also hurt the people and animals that drink or use[75] the water.

Water should be cleaned before it is used. Water is filtered to get rid of bad chemicals. Filtered water is safe for drinking and cooking.[102]

Water and Us

Write words that will help you remember what you learned.

Water in Your Life

_____
_____
_____
_____

Fresh or Salty?

_____
_____
_____
_____

Water in the Air

_____
_____
_____
_____

The Water Cycle

_____
_____
_____
_____

Clean Water

_____
_____
_____
_____

Water in Your Life

1. "Water in Your Life" is MAINLY about ____
   - Ⓐ all the water in the classroom.
   - Ⓑ how important water is.
   - Ⓒ why we drink water.
   - Ⓓ how much water animals need.

2. Why do people need water?

_____

_____

_____

Fresh or Salty?

1. Another good name for "Fresh or Salty?" is ____
   - Ⓐ "Water in the Oceans."
   - Ⓑ "Finding Drinking Water."
   - Ⓒ "Too Little Water."
   - Ⓓ "Two Kinds of Water."

2. Why should people use fresh water carefully?

_____

_____

_____

Water and Us

Water in the Air

1. What are three forms of water?

Ⓐ steam, water vapor, boiling water

Ⓑ water, ice, water vapor

Ⓒ water vapor, ice, boiling water

Ⓓ water vapor, steam, water

2. What is steam?

_____

_____

_____

The Water Cycle

1. What is the main idea of "The Water Cycle"?

Ⓐ Water is used again and again.

Ⓑ New water is made all the time.

Ⓒ Water in rain is new water.

Ⓓ Water from the sky is called water vapor.

2. What are the steps in the water cycle?

_____

_____

_____

Clean Water

1. The main idea of "Clean Water" is that ____

   Ⓐ all water is safe.

   Ⓑ chemicals do not easily mix with water.

   Ⓒ water does not mix easily with other things.

   Ⓓ water must be cleaned so it is safe to use.

2. Why should bad chemicals be taken out of water?

_____

_____

_____

Connect Your Ideas

1. Name three ways you use water every day.

_____

_____

_____

2. Suppose there was another reading. Do you think it would be about rain or farms? Why?

_____

_____

_____

Rocks

Rocks are all around us, on land and under the water.

Rocks Around You

Even if you are reading this on a boat on water, there is rock below you. When you look down, you may[25] see a rug, dirt, grass, or water. Yet under the rug, dirt, grass, or water, there is rock.

When you look at some rocks, you[50] see different colors. Every color is a different mineral. Other rocks are only one color. These rocks are made up of just one mineral. Minerals[75] are different from plants and animals. They are not alive like plants and animals. Rocks are made when water and heat act on Earth over thousands of years.[103]

This picture shows hardened lava on a road.

How Are Rocks Made?

You can tell by looking at a rock how it was made. Rocks with layers were made under water. The water[25] that flows into lakes and seas has dirt in it. As the dirt sinks into the lake or sea, the new dirt pushes down on[50] older dirt. Over thousands of years, the layers of dirt get very hard.

Rocks with black and white grains or ones that look like black[75] glass were made by heat. In a volcano, minerals flow out of the earth as lava. When the lava from a volcano cools, the minerals harden to become rocks.[104]

Rocks

The moon is a big rock that
we can see from far away.

Big and Small, Hard and Soft

A grain of sand is so small you might not see it. The moon is so big that you[25] can see it from thousands of miles away. A grain of sand and the moon are different sizes. Yet both are rocks.

Rocks are different[50] in how soft or hard they are. Diamonds are the hardest rocks. The only thing that is hard enough to cut a diamond is another[75] diamond. Talc is a very soft rock. Talc is so soft that it is used as a powder for babies. Diamonds and talc are very different rocks.[102]

The picture shows salt that has
been taken from seawater.

A Rock We Eat

When you put salt on your food, you are eating small parts of a rock. Salt is a mineral that is[25] found in seawater. Rocks made of salt are found where seas used to be. The water from these seas dried up, but the salt was[50] left behind.

Salt has many uses. Salt can make some foods taste better. Many years ago, people did not have ways to freeze food. They[75] kept their food from rotting with salt. Salt was so important that it was even used as money. People traded salt for the things they needed.[101]

Rocks

What things made from rocks
do you see in this classroom?

Uses of Rocks

People use rocks in many ways. Look around your classroom. Are there bricks in the walls? Bricks are made from rocks. Are[25] there windows in your classroom? The glass in windows is made mostly from sand. Sand is little bits of rocks.

You use two things in[50] school every day that are made from rocks. These two things are chalk and pencils. The chalk that you use when you write on the[75] board is a rock. Even the board used to be made of rock. When you write with a pencil, you are writing with part of a rock, too.[103]

 **Rocks**

Write words that will help you remember what you learned.

Rocks Around You

_____

_____

_____

_____

How Are Rocks Made?

_____

_____

_____

_____

Big and Small, Hard and Soft

_____

_____

_____

_____

A Rock We Eat

_____

_____

_____

_____

Uses of Rocks

_____

_____

_____

_____

Rocks Around You

1. Where are the rocks on Earth?

   Ⓐ on land and under the water

   Ⓑ in grass and dirt

   Ⓒ under the water

   Ⓓ in minerals

2. What are rocks made of?

_____

_____

_____

How Are Rocks Made?

1. "How Are Rocks Made?" is MAINLY about _____

   Ⓐ the way rocks are made.

   Ⓑ different kinds of rocks.

   Ⓒ rocks in volcanoes.

   Ⓓ rocks from long ago.

2. What are two ways rocks are made?

_____

_____

_____

 **Rocks**

Big and Small, Hard and Soft

1. How are grains of sand and the moon alike?

    Ⓐ Both are soft.

    Ⓑ Both are hard to cut.

    Ⓒ Both are rocks.

    Ⓓ Both are very hard.

2. How can rocks be different from one another?

_____

_____

_____

A Rock We Eat

1. Another good name for "A Rock We Eat" is ____

    Ⓐ "How to Make Salt."

    Ⓑ "Freezing Food."

    Ⓒ "The Rock Named Salt."

    Ⓓ "Salt Used as Money."

2. What are three ways salt has been used?

_____

_____

_____

Uses of Rocks

1. The main idea of "Uses of Rocks" is _____

   (A) how people use rocks.

   (B) how rocks are used in homes.

   (C) where people find rocks.

   (D) how people use bricks and glass.

2. What are two ways you use rocks in school?

   _____

   _____

   _____

Connect Your Ideas

1. Name four ways you use rocks every day.

   _____

   _____

   _____

2. What rock that you read about do you use most? Why?

   _____

   _____

   _____

Reading Log · Level B · Book 2

	I Read This	New Words I Learned	New Facts I Learned	What Else I Want to Learn About This Subject
Maps				
What Is a Map?				
A Map to Your House				
Keys to Maps				
Different Maps				
Mapmaking				
Money				
What Is Money?				
Different Kinds of Money				
Coins				
Paper Money				
Bankcards				
Jobs Around Us				
Jobs That Help You				
Keeping Us Safe				
Building New Things				
Keeping Track of Money				
Bringing Us Food				

	I Read This	New Words I Learned	New Facts I Learned	What Else I Want to Learn About This Subject
Weather				
Weather Around You				
Wind				
Clouds and Fog				
Rain or Snow?				
Climate				
Water and Us				
Water in Your Life				
Fresh or Salty?				
Water in the Air				
The Water Cycle				
Clean Water				
Rocks				
Rocks Around You				
How Are Rocks Made?				
Big and Small, Hard and Soft				
A Rock We Eat				
Uses of Rocks				

Self-Check Graph

Mark your reading rate here.

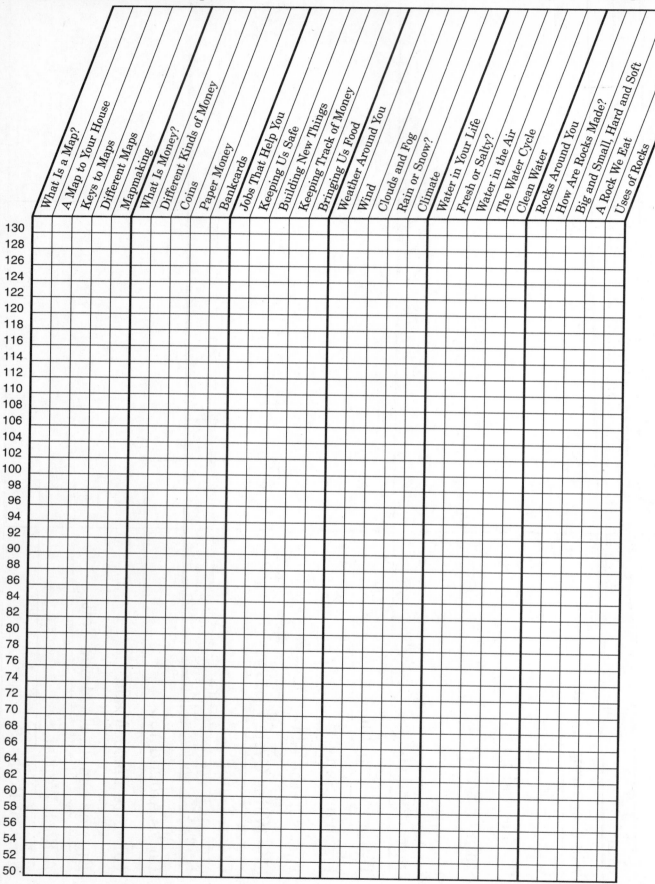

Column headers (left to right):
What Is a Map?, A Map to Your House, Keys to Maps, Different Maps, Mapmaking, What Is Money?, Different Kinds of Money, Coins, Paper Money, Bankcards, Jobs That Help You, Keeping Us Safe, Building New Things, Keeping Track of Money, Bringing Us Food, Weather Around You, Wind, Clouds and Fog, Rain or Snow?, Climate, Water in Your Life, Fresh or Salty?, Water in the Air, The Water Cycle, Clean Water, Rocks Around You, How Are Rocks Made?, Big and Small, Hard and Soft, A Rock We Eat, Uses of Rocks

Row values (left axis): 130, 128, 126, 124, 122, 120, 118, 116, 114, 112, 110, 108, 106, 104, 102, 100, 98, 96, 94, 92, 90, 88, 86, 84, 82, 80, 78, 76, 74, 72, 70, 68, 66, 64, 62, 60, 58, 56, 54, 52, 50